"Christian Marriage 101"

"Tips for a Healthy Marriage"

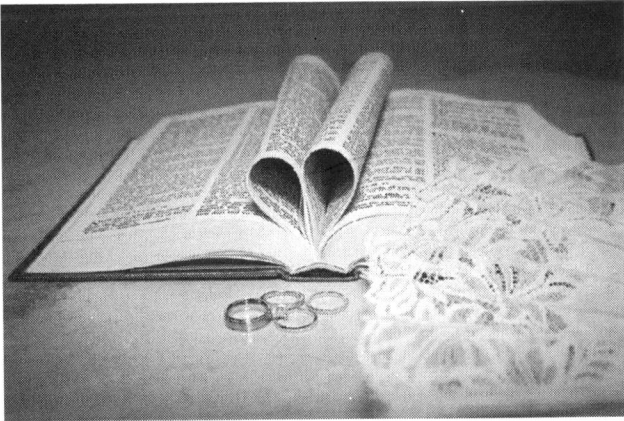

By: Pastor Joey Bauer

A Publication of Comeback Kids Ministries.

www.comebackkids.webs.com

www.pastorjoeybauer.org

www.facebook.com/cbk217

i

BLOOD

SWEAT

TEARS

Facebook.com/CBK217

Comebackkids.webs.com

I want to dedicate this book to one person and only one person. It is the person who deals with my wonderful mess of a life, shares her life with me and has taught me how to love to the best of my ability. She has taught me that no matter what happens in life, a marriage can last, and be happy with a little bit of elbow grease. Thank you Janielle, my Beloved. I love you.

Love your messy, crazy hubby.

Joey!!!

Table of Contents:

Everybody wants to know what the master key is to a great marriage, in this chapter we will discuss what it is and how to do it properly.

The power of Good thoughts!

Marriage is a commitment, not just a simple agreement but a commitment.

Some final thoughts from the heart of Pastor Joey.

Introduction

"Why I wrote this Book."

Genesis 2: 18-24

[18] And the Lord God said, It is not good that the man should be alone; I will make him an help meet for him.

[19] And out of the ground the Lord God formed every beast of the field, and every fowl of the air; and brought them unto Adam to see what he would call them: and whatsoever Adam called every living creature, that was the name thereof.

[20] And Adam gave names to all cattle, and to the fowl of the air, and to every beast of the field; but for Adam there was not found an help meet for him.

21 And the Lord God caused a deep sleep to fall upon Adam, and he slept: and he took one of his ribs, and closed up the flesh instead thereof;

22 And the rib, which the Lord God had taken from man, made he a woman, and brought her unto the man.

23 And Adam said, This is now bone of my bones, and flesh of my flesh: she shall be called Woman, because she was taken out of Man.

24 Therefore shall a man leave his father and his mother, and shall cleave unto his wife: and they shall be one flesh.

Before I go on and on about why I wrote this book, I want to point out something amazing about the Bible scripture we just read from Genesis chapter 2. You will notice that God saw that man was alone, and he must have seen that Man longed for companionship in the form of a wife, so God created Eve to as his "Help meet," which simply means a person who helps, or in my words, a person who helps to "Pick up the slack." Even though this is important and we will pick up more on this later in the book, I wanted you to see that even though Man was made from the ground and the dirt, Eve was made from the rib in Adams side. The reason for this (As I believe) is because Eve (Women) was never meant to walk in front of men, nor was she ever meant to be following the back of men, but rather she should always be attached to his side from where the rib was taken. Our wives roles are not to play follow the leader or as some would say "Wear the Pants" and charge out in front of man, but rather to be at our sides as the lovely "Help meet" God created with purpose and dignity.

Now I must say that I have done my fair share of marriage counseling being in the field of psychology and Christian Ministry, but I want everybody to know that I am far from an expert in this field, well let me rephrase that... I am a semi-expert but only who learned everything the hard way. IN my "Trial by fire" refining route I went through I learned a lot about what you should and should not do in a marriage or even in a relationship.

I have been married three times. Yes you heard that right, "Three times." The first time I was young, very young, and ambitious and I met the girl of my dreams only for the marriage to be torn apart by an ugly terminal illness and other situations that presented themselves. I was so distraught about the way things went with the "Love of my life" that I was a lonely mess, and I jumped into another relationship trying to fix that problem. It didn't fix anything and only made myself and the person who I was married to, hate each other. Even though she and I get along now, and I can honestly say she is a great person, we went through a period where we took out our emotional misery on each other. We went through horrible court trials, a long messy divorce and a lot of regrets which led me to really think about myself, my own failures, what I should have done, and shouldn't have done. It really made me think about the value of a marriage and what God can do when he is the center of a marriage. Now I do think if I had the knowledge then that I have now, I, and my previous partner probably could have made it last and stick together but I didn't know then what I know now. This is why I feel compelled to write down all my failures and triumphs in hopes that it helps even just a handful of people. I can honestly say that everything I talk about in this book has been lived the hard way by me, tried and tested, trusted and true. These things in my past have helped me in my current marriage to whom I believe is my soul mate, because her and I have taken courses in life that seem very similar and we both have an understanding of what "Not to do" and "What to do" in a marriage. I am not going to lie and say it's easy, marriage is hard. Really hard! Dating is easy. The butterflies we get, the wonderful date nights with your potential lifelong partner, the romantic gestures as well as the amazing times you have smiling, laughing and discovering one another, it's all the easy part of a relationship. The day comes though when you say your vows, kiss your Hunny, and then take your honeymoon, but then you wake up the next morning, listening to your partner snore, or smelling the bad breath from that romantic seafood dinner the night of your wedding and you think to yourself, "Oh my gosh! Who is this person in my bed!?"

I know it seems funny as you read but it is so, so true. We think about what in the heck we just got ourselves into and then we start seeing the little things they do that we thought at one time were so cute and endearing, but we see them and start to get irritated and mad. Things as small as how they roll up the toothpaste container, put the toilet paper roll on, to things as big as their compulsive shopping habits, and loud burping we once thought was just an amazing quality. Oh boy if I only knew then what I know now, haha! I would actually still be married but more prepared. I understand that marriage is hard and at times something as little as a message from a pastor, or a passage in a book can be the make or break on if the marriage last.

In today's world marriage is actually near impossible and we are seeing a growing trend even among Christians that shows people have devalued the meaning of marriage and what God once created to help us in our lives has become a burden that many are either stuck in unhappily or they chose to just never do. I read that 50% of the marriages in America end within the first 5 years of the institution with a big Divorce sign plastered on it. An even sadder statistic I read around the same time, in the same article is that the divorce rate among Christians is at least a third higher than the divorce rate among secular marriages. Why are so many believer choosing to end their marriages? There are many reasons. T.V. and Magazines show men what their women should look like, which in reality is never going to happen because the way sex and the body is portrayed on these things is far from the real deal. Men have been deceived by the enemy that their wife must look like a top rated swim suit model or else he should move on to the next thing. Another reason is because women have been indoctrinated on how men should be, and behave. If they haven't been indoctrinated by this they see how a "players" and a "cheaters" life is portrayed in today's society and they don't want any part of it. It's a sad, sad reality that marriage, beauty, and even character is being twisted into a mockery by the world and the Church has fallen prey to its devices. We see women and men both growing up wanting to meet their prince charming or fairytale princess, well I hate to break it to you boys and girls, there is no fairytale or prince charming coming your way. Marriage isn't what you see it is on the Disney channel or old shows on Nick at Night like "Leave it to Beaver" and the "Brady Bunch." It's just not the reality. Now don't get me wrong, it can become the reality but you have to work at it. You have to build it, and you have to fight for it.

So my goal with this book is to show you small tips and tricks that I have learned so you can fight better to keep your marriage alive, strong and healthy. To give you some tools to help build that dream you had as a child and to give you the knowledge and know how to work your butt off and not settle for anything less than a newspaper column about you and your spouse's 65th anniversary. Oh yes, this all can happen, but not overnight and not without work. What is it your parents, coaches and teachers would tell you growing up, "Anything is possible if you work hard to achieve it." I hope after you have gotten done readings this small book, that you have at least gained some hope that if you have Jesus in your marriage, then you can have that happily ever after you always wanted. I love you guys and wish you the best on your journey to beating the statistics of this world, who ever wanted to just be a number anyway?

Chapter 1

"Priorities, Priorities!"

Matthew 6: 33

[33] But seek ye first the kingdom of God, and his righteousness; and all these things shall be added unto you.

We must realize that God always comes first in a Christian relationship, after that, your Spouse comes second. Kids will always come AFTER your wife or husband and then everything else falls after these three things. We must honor God in everything as well as keeping the protocol of marriage which is always GOD FIRST, SPOUSE SECOND, KIDS THIRD. The place of God in a family must not be uncertain or shaky. God should hold the position of a father to everyone including the husband. He occupies the position of that supernatural power that can be counted on when all human strengths and efforts do fail and the wife and children must understand this from the husband's relationship with the Father, God. It is in putting God first that the foundations of love and understanding which God commands us to live by can thrive. Keeping God first means keeping His laws and ordinances. A child that has learned to put God first by studying the word of God as in the bible and living by it is therefore less given to being disobedient, lying or other vices that are propagated by the devil. A child that has learnt that God is first in his life and that of his family knows that God is in absolute control of all situations and would rather pray in hard times than blame his/her parents for not being able to salvage a situation or embrace vices of today's society. Same applies to the wife in a family that puts God first. It would help her understand that her husband is the head of the family by God's authority. When a husband keeps God first, it's easier for him to love his wife and children, for God is love and commands us to Love the same. It is easier for him to keep the family in that "togetherness" of love, understanding and peace. Same it is for a wife who is nurtured by her love for God as she would be submissive to her husband realizing that her husband is the representative of God, that they can see in that family. If anything else takes the place of God in a family, in other words, if a family gives God a second seat, it is impossible for God to take control of the affairs of such a family. There can never be two captains in a ship and God can never be second fiddle to any person or thing. It is either we let him take total control of our lives and in this case the family or we are more or less piloting our affairs ourselves; and how much can we do to weather the storms of life? Most importantly, making heaven is impossible should anything else take the place of God in our lives or our family.

Another thing we must realize is that only in God can we find the love we so crave. Yes, we get married because we love a certain somebody, but perfect love can only be accomplished by God the Father. Only Jesus can offer you that PERFECT love. Our spouses are supposed to try to follow the guidelines depicted in 1 Corinthians 13, but your spouse will always fall short. When He/She falls short we can only find refuge in God. Your wife breaks your heart, maybe she isn't patient with you like she should be, but it's ok because we can find that patience in God. Maybe your husband has a drinking problem and you can't trust his actions, its ok, there is no need to fret because when you said your vows in the sight of God you gave him preeminence over your marriage and you can trust God with your husband. Trust God, put him first. This is how we find peace in our marriages and heal the wounds that this world's type of love has left in our relationships. Maybe your husband has been unfaithful, maybe the person reading this book has been unfaithful in their marriage, it's not the end if you give your marriage over to God and trust in his Faithfulness. I have seen God do mighty things when a spouse decides to put him first.

I remember one man in a church I served at some years ago, was going through a divorce. He and his wife had gone their separate ways and the divorce trials had lasted for about a year. The man did not want a divorce, and he cried to God for a restoration to take place, but for a whole year he had to endure the pain of trial after trial, adding up the bills, splitting the belongings, and even child custody decisions, but we all remained in pray with him and he stood for God, put him first and then one morning he went into what was going to be the trial that finalized everything. He looked into the judge's eyes and was sore afraid, but he continued to keep God first in his heart and to remember the Lords promises. All of a sudden his soon to be ex-wife, asked the judge if she and her attorney could have a few moments with this man and his attorney. The judge gave them some time. As soon as they entered the adjacent room the women wrapped her arms around her husband and told him she was sorry. She told him this was a mistake and she didn't want to go through with the divorce. Still to this day this marriage is strong, they continue to put God first in every aspect and when one of them messes up and fails to live up to their end of the marriage bargain, instead of getting mad, they keep God first, pick up each other's slack and keep moving in a forward direction. Very rarely is a marriage working with both partners at 100% all day, every day. I used to hear people say that if a person who was married wasn't always putting in 100% than they would end up divorced, but in all honesty there are many things that keep a marriage partner from operating at 100% all the time. First off, we are all human, our bodies get exhausted, tired, and even lazy. Our bodies get sick on us. Some of us have to work two jobs to make the rent, others like pastors are always having to give as much as they can to their congregations. Maybe you are in a marriage where you have two kids, you both work, and have to play full time everything. Very, very rarely do we always, any single one of us put 100% into our marriage. This is where the importance of "For better or for worse" and the rest of your marriage vows come in. You and your spouse are partners, in these times of stress where you might be putting out 100% and your spouse is only operating at 50%, this is not where you start to complain, worry, stress or get angry, NO!!! This is where you actually become each other's help mates and pick up each other's slack. So many times I have wanted to put into a marriage vow, and ceremony, "Do you Kira, promise to always pick up Kevin's slack? For better or worse, in sickness and in health?" Now… "Do you Kevin promise to pick up Kira's slack, for better or worse, in sickness and in health? Till death do you part?" I always wanted to say that because it is so true. We must be realistic and down to Earth about these things. By the way, I only use the names of Kevin and Kira because it was a wedding I did that I will never forget. Two beautiful people, high school sweet hearts getting married on their ranch. I hope they read this book and remember that beautiful day, and cherish it… Even after picking up so much of each other's slack, I was joking of course so I hope they don't get offended. I love you guys, but back to the topic. We must always remember that even though we can't always put out 100% into our marriages, God will always see the promises you made to one another, cherish it, remember it, and he will always give you 100% of his time, attention, and Love. KEEP GOD FIRST, above all else, and you will be ok.

Chapter 2

"Making the Ultimate Choice!"

Deuteronomy 7: 6-9

⁶ For thou art an holy people unto the Lord thy God: the Lord thy God hath chosen thee to be a special people unto himself, above all people that are upon the face of the earth.

⁷ The Lord did not set his love upon you, nor choose you, because ye were more in number than any people; for ye were the fewest of all people:

⁸ But because the Lord loved you, and because he would keep the oath which he had sworn unto your fathers, hath the Lord brought you out with a mighty hand, and redeemed you out

of the house of bondmen, from the hand of Pharaoh king of Egypt.

⁹ Know therefore that the Lord thy God, he is God, the faithful God, which keepeth covenant and mercy with them that love him and keep his commandments to a thousand generations;

What I wanted to bring out in this setting of Scripture is how God loves us, it is the exact way he expects us to Love others, especially our spouses. Although it is often felt in the heart, love is primarily an act of the will. Nowhere is this demonstrated more clearly than in the way God loves us. In the Old Testament, two Hebrew words describe God's love for his people. The first Hebrew word for love, "*ahab,*" means: "to desire, to breathe after; to be inclined toward, to delight in." The Lord God delights in us and is inclined toward us. He desires "breathes after" us with affectionate (ahab) love. Although Ahab is an intense word, it's only used a handful of times with regard to the Lord. There's another richer, more powerful word that's used repeatedly throughout Old Testament Scripture to describe God's love for us: the Hebrew word "*chesed*."

"*Chesed*" speaks of a love that is firmly rooted in choice. It involves loyalty, steadfastness and commitment to a promise. It's a love that doesn't depend on the response or behavior of the receiver but rather on the steadfast character and commitment of the giver. "*Ahab*" has to do with feelings, whereas "*chesed*" implies a mind-set and mode of interaction based on unwavering loyalty to a commitment.

"Always remember that love is a choice."

Understand that Love is a Choice, LOVE IS A CHOICE, it is not merely a feeling or an emotion. If you fall in love... You made that choice. If you fall out of love, then again you made the choice to fall out of love. You have to choose to love, even when it's hard. Love is not conditional. What the world calls love today is indeed not true. Love in its truest sense is agape. It does not discontinue because a loved one's finances are no longer promising or because a partner is not in the best of health conditions. Once you have made that vow; said "I do", you don't get to revoke it; it's not a contract. That is why the Bible says that "For this reason a man will leave his father and mother and cling to his wife. When you agreed to love your wife or husband and vowed to love him or her in good times and in bad times, in sickness and in health and for richer or poorer, it was sealed as a covenant of marriage as ordained by God which cannot be broken.

One must choose to love one's spouse no matter the circumstances and yes, there may be tough times, but how we choose to react to these is what matters the most. We must choose to love because with this same love has Christ loved us that even though we stray and ignore his sacrifice and throw the grace of salvation he offers us in his face again and again, he still gives us a chance to begin with him all over again each time. I once watched the movie titled "Fireproof" and had to get it for keeps, it made me reflect on my own marriage and things I wasn't doing right. It helped me realize that if I wanted change in my marriage (Howbeit Happiness and joy) then it would be up to me to take the first steps to create it. We cannot keep blaming each other in our marriages, we must take responsibility of our own actions and go from there. For example, how many times can we say, He did this or she did that, AND THAT IS WHY I CANT DO THINGS THE RIGHT WAY! They are provoking me! We hear that all the time right? Just as love is a choice, it is also a choice on how you handle a situation. You are always in control of your own actions. Jesus said if we get slapped in the face, then we should turn our other cheek to get slapped as well. This is how marriage works, we may get slapped a bunch of times, but if we endure and pray, we will eventually see our marriages turned around... I recommend every married couple watches "Fireproof" and reflects it on their own lives, not your spouse's life, your own life. We can only work on ourselves. It is a story of how unconditional love conquers. Even when it gets hard and it seems your spouse does not see all you do to make your marriage work, you must keep on. Even if the marriage seems dead, lifeless and like it is never going to come back to its former glory.

There is no limit at which you should stop because getting a divorce doesn't make you free from the promise you made, but rather a promise breaker of a commitment you made. Remember in the Gospels, Jesus was cornered and asked if a woman should be put away because of certain wrongs, they asked if the husband should divorce his wife according to the Law of Moses and Jesus told them the truth... He stated that "It was only because of the hardness of your hearts" that Moses had that as a writ, but what God has joined together, let no man put asunder. God hates Divorce. It is a breach in the institution he set up. Divorce can be avoided so easily but because of the hardness of our hearts we want to start over, we don't want to forgive and the most crucial part of forgiveness is forgetfulness. We would rather become bitter than forgive. We will let our pride well up and begin fighting about who does what, how this gets done, who the provider is and trivial things. When pride wells up God can't perform the healing needed to mend the broken and bitter hearts. I am convinced that ANY marriage can be worked out is we just made the choice to love no matter what. Agape Love, Supreme love, the Love that can only be inspired by Jesus who gives us the power to love this way.

Sometimes we must choose to love even in the worst, when our husbands have cheated, or our wives have been unfaithful, when we've been lied to, beat up and broken by the one we trusted so much we must still find the strength to choose to love and be committed to the commitment we made. Sometimes we can become so bitter that we cannot commit to our spouse so I encourage you to be committed to the commitment of the marriage vows you took. So choose to love your spouse in all circumstances. It's in so doing and dialoguing that you can reach each other's hearts. Why do the strongest virtues always seem the weakest? Like the power of unwavering love in the face of rejection. Keep loving even when you get none in return.

Always remember that "Love is patient and kind. It is never jealous. Love is neither boastful nor conceited. It is never rude or selfish; it does not take offence and is not resentful. Love takes no pleasure in other people's sins, but delights in the truth. It is

always ready to excuse, to trust, to
hope and to endure whatever comes."

Chapter 3

"Let no man (NOTHING) put Asunder!"

Matthew 19: 3-8

³ The Pharisees also came unto him, tempting him, and saying unto him, Is it lawful for a man to put away his wife for every cause?

⁴ And he answered and said unto them, Have ye not read, that he which made them at the beginning made them male and female,

⁵ And said, For this cause shall a man leave father and mother, and shall cleave to his wife: and they twain shall be one flesh?

⁶ Wherefore they are no more twain, but one flesh. What therefore God hath joined together, let not man put asunder.

7 They say unto him, Why did Moses then command to give a writing of divorcement, and to put her away?

8 He saith unto them, Moses because of the hardness of your hearts suffered you to put away your wives: but from the beginning it was not so.

Don't let anybody, anything, or any feeling come between you and your spouse: So many things want to try to take control of us and make us put it before our spouses. Family can cause division. Friends can cause division, jobs, possessions, and even feelings. Don't let it happen. In marriage, the influence of your extended family on the course of your marriage should be limited. Be well bound to your spouse and let your spouse be your number one confidant. You must keep nothing hidden from each other. Never act on information given to you about your spouse without talking to your spouse about it first. Engage in non – confrontational dialogue. This way, distrust will not build up between you and your spouse over information which may be misleading. Many a happy marriage has been made sour by the seed of discord sown by external parties. When I say external parties, do not expect strangers you don't know or someone you run into on the road. It is those close to you. It could be family members, relations or friends. They are friends of the family alright but it must be ensured that they don't come in between, either trying to help you make things right in your marriage, tell you a wrong they have discovered your spouse is given to or how to better your union with your spouse. They may mean well but do not have them come between; it is a union between two people, just you and your spouse.

Another is realizing the place of our jobs and career and ensuring it does not interfere with our roles in the family. Our work schedule must be well defined. We may be tempted to work late hours due to set targets that have to be met but it is easier to stand on our prior decision if we have our time schedule well defined from the onset. Have a set time at which you must be home to be with your family; to appreciate your spouse and get to be with your children. Many an executive these days leave in the early hours of the day before the kids are up from bed in the bid to beat the traffic and be at work on time. Added to this, we end up working extra hours after closing time to get that top exec presentation slated for the next day ready only to return home late when the kids are already in bed and to meet a disappointed spouse who had to eat a cold meal alone after waiting for hours for our return. This is just a scenario of work getting between one and one's spouse. If not nipped in the bud, this has the potential to metamorphose into a catastrophe, estranging one from one's kids. In the 21st century, this does not only refer to the men who are most often the ones caught up in this but also goes out to working class wives. When we understand how important succeeding in our home front is, we would not sacrifice it on an altar of our job's demands.

Now, before you get me wrong... Because I said I wanted to be realistic and truthful with this book, we know that at times our jobs do get in the way, work has to get done and as my wife says... "Hunny, the dishes don't do themselves." How well versed with wisdom my wife is, with her hint of sarcasm... But we know that at time, no matter how hard it may be, we must be away on a business trip, or as most preachers will admit to, Church gets in the way of a million other obligations so my advice to every married couple, especially the ones with kids it that you remember the following.

MOMMY NEEDS MOMMY TIME:

Being a wife and mother is hard, and we all ned time to ourselves to do what we would like to do whether it be writing, other hobbies or just chilling in bed, eating Oreos and watching Millionaire Matchmaker. Mommy will always need time to herself.

DADDY NEEDS DADDY TIME:

Just like Mommy, Husband and Daddy needs his time with the boys, fishing, working on cars, and maybe even some boxing matches with old friends on a cement slab in a park somewhere... Manly right? Maybe not, but the same is true with men. We need our time as well.

MOMMY AND DADDY NEED MOMMY AND DADDY TIME:

It's ok to take your wife on dates even after you are married. Make up a time, even set up an appointment if you have to, to woo your partner all over again just like you two did when you were dating. It is so important that this doesn't get neglected or else a family will crumble from the top down. With this being said, INTIMACY comes into play. You will never imagine how many marriages I have seen suffer because of the lack of a sex life. God made us to enjoy our spouse and their bodies in the bedroom. I blame the main stream Christian Church for this as well because for so long the Church has deemed talking about sex as a bad thing, but it is so important. I can even write a whole new book just on this topic but ill keep it short and sweet here in this section with some do's and don'ts of sex. A husband or wife should NEVER withhold their bodies from one another, Paul talks about it in the Gospels. Sex should never be used as a bargaining chip, deal maker or breaker, and the bedroom should be a place where both the husband and wife feel free with their spouse, inhibited, and not afraid to share each other's bodies with one another. Men, remember that for us, sex begins in the kitchen. Women work so differently than us men do. They need mental stimulation, a show of appreciation even if it's doing the dishes or cooking dinner. Woo your wife my friends and you will never be unsatisfied. Now women, what you must do is ALWAYS BE AVAILABLE.

Seriously, that's it. Now I will admit, it's a secret that us men don't want to let out but we like to be pursued as well, we like the kisses from out of nowhere and the public displays of affection too but most of the time it just comes down to being their when he needs you. Now I do understand that there are things that can affect this, like past sexual abuse or other mental health disorders, life crises, and things out of our control but all you need to remember is that Jesus never expected us to be perfect, he just wanted us to give it our best shot, so just try my friends and go from there. But it all comes down to this, that Mommy and Daddy need time just for themselves, and its not a selfish thing either.

FAMILY WILL ALWAYS NEED FAMILY TIME:

A family that prays together stays together. Have you ever heard this? Well the same is true with a family that goes to eat dinner together, goes to the movies together, the park together, and to church together. The family unit as a whole can never be neglected or else your children will never be whole. Make sure to never neglect your family time.

MOMMY NEEDS TIME WITH THE KIDS, AND DADDY NEEDS TIME WITH THE KIDS:

I have seen so many children grow up into dysfunctional adults because dad never took Mike fishing, or because Mom never had those motherly bonds with Jessica, so Jessica and Mike grow up with a whole part of their lives missing. Children need a father figure in their lives and they need to spend time with them, just as Children need a strong mother figure in their lives and need to spend time with them. It is so sad how the world is down playing the role of a father, or a mother, when in all honesty this is where the path to being a positive member of the community starts. Never in my life, except now have I seen so many parents give up all together and give their kids up because they don't want to give up an addiction, a dysfunctional relationship or a way of life. It is time for Men and Women to stand up and do the right thing. I worked as a contracted worker with Child Protective Services in a unit that was called Differential Response.

It was a program meant to help families who have been in and out of the CPS system attain help in whatever form we can help them. Whether it was community programs, help with court, paperwork, or connecting them with people who could help. It is a great program and has helped so many people who use the help, but sadly while working in this system I saw parents who just didn't care anymore as well. Sadly these cases would end up being taken back to the court system and removing the child, all because a man or a women somewhere couldn't stand up and do the right thing by cleaning up their lives and raising their child. This is where we who know to do the right thing come into play. The people who keep time with their families because we will raise children who contribute to those who never had a chance. We as moms and dads have the joy of raising a child who could be the next Mayor, Governor, or President. We could be raising a child who finds the final cure for cancer, or who puts an end to world hunger. Please my friends, always make time for your family. But back to the point of all of this, not letting anything come between our marriages.

At some other times it is even something else that comes between one and one's spouse not people or jobs now. It could be the desire for something, the strife involved in trying to get something one wants when gone after at all cost. Having to be without something which one desires strongly, sometimes affects peoples mood. Things like not getting a promotion that one feels that one deserves, losing out on a business deal, a contract or the sorts. These should not come between married couples. As Christians, we should first and foremost, realize that no material desire or craving should be a do or die affair for us. We must not worry for want of anything so much that it affects our relationship with our spouse. Sometimes, we see cases of frustrations arising from failure at something, being carried home and the aggressions transferred to an unsuspecting spouse. If indeed we believe that we serve Jehovah Jireh – "God our provider," then we need not allow strife and worry to deny our marriage the joy we well deserve. What is important is to trust that God is sure to make yours whatever belongs to you and is able to give you whatever is within his will for your life. Hence when in such situations, what is required of us is to relay same to our spouse and pray about it together and then trust that God will make good his promises. The knowledge that worrying about these things will not change the circumstances is vital here. Just like the bible states, who among you has by worrying added an inch to the hair on his/her head? Anything or feeling that brings you down, makes you bitter or vengeful has the potential to affect your relationship with your spouse. Try to eschew them.

Next is drug abuse or alcohol. Illicit drug and excessive drinking does no one any good. In marriage, it seriously affects ones relationship with a spouse and its devastating effect is so enormous it could well drag down both spouses emotionally. Like other addictive tendencies, its best to keep it out than let it in and then fight to discontinue. The bouts of depression could cripple all communication and trust. Added to this is the financial decline that it brings along. Gambling, pornography and the sorts of all addictive tendencies must not be allowed into our lives as Christians. As a Christian, you are expected to see only your spouse's nakedness. Watching pornographic films under any excuses or recommendations is not biblical and is an absolute No, No.

In all, we should not allow anything to come between us and our spouse. We should not allow anybody or anything

to cause discord between us and our
life long partners.

Chapter 4

"Making a Plan!"

Luke 14: 28-32

[28] For which of you, intending to build a tower, sitteth not down first, and counteth the cost, whether he have sufficient to finish it?

[29] Lest haply, after he hath laid the foundation, and is not able to finish it, all that behold it begin to mock him,

[30] Saying, This man began to build, and was not able to finish.

[31] Or what king, going to make war against another king, sitteth not down first, and consulteth whether he be able with ten thousand to meet him that cometh against him with twenty thousand?

32 Or else, while the other is yet a great way off, he sendeth an ambassage, and desireth conditions of peace.

Have a "Mission Statement" for your marriage and family. Write down somewhere the goals you want your marriage and family to achieve and be there for each other to help the family unit get there. There should be a vision and short term goals, set to enable the family to work on and achieve these goals in the family which will bring that long term vision to fruition step by step. It is always advisable to write down your goals, though they are short term, they are very imperative for keep where we are going with our families in focus. Every decision made in t should be purposeful and taken to achieve an expected end which must be within a God driven purpose.

There is a saying that goes thus "If you don't know where you are going, you will never get there." It is therefore important that we plan where we want to be, what needs to be done to get there and when. This makes it easier to get things done right, track progress and to know when things start going wrong because most times what we have is a problem of not knowing when things started going wrong. Most couples just find that it seems they just woke up and the problems were all there overnight. Some couples argue that their marriage has been going good for the most part but that suddenly, things started going awry. It doesn't happen all of a sudden. We must be there supporting each other to ensure that the goals of the units of the family becomes a success. If from the offset, you desire to give your children an Ivy League education, then you need to initiate your spouse on this and then save and plan towards it; you want your relationship with your spouse to be as romantic as your honeymoon days even during your celebration of your silver jubilee (50 years for those who didn't know what a Silver Jubilee was, like I didn't before I researched)?

Then be ready to put in the extra work. Have dates scheduled on which you take just her out for a treat which you don't miss, send her flowers and let her know you love her just as much as when you first got married.

Do you want your children to be God fearing? Then you need to have a plan on how to make that achievable. You will have to decide which schools to enroll them in, putting how morals is handled in different schools into consideration. Then you should perhaps apportion quiet time for them, have scheduled family morning devotion and again joint evening devotion just before bed. For the family you dream of to come to be, all these has to be planned and structured out and not left to chance. You must pray and ask for God's guidance in laying the foundations and ground rules that would facilitate this.

Chapter 5

"The good Stuff!"

Philippians 4: 6-8

[6] Be careful for nothing; but in every thing by prayer and supplication with thanksgiving let your requests be made known unto God.

[7] And the peace of God, which passeth all understanding, shall keep your hearts and minds through Christ Jesus.

[8] Finally, brethren, whatsoever things are true, whatsoever things are honest, whatsoever things are just, whatsoever things are pure, whatsoever things are lovely, whatsoever things are of good report; if there be any virtue, and if there be any praise, think on these things.

Have you ever heard that song by Kenny Chesney, "The good stuff?" Just so you don't have to stop everything and take a listen I'll explain a little. It was about a man and a women who got into a fight, the man went to the bar and asked for a drink, but the bartender instead gave him a glass of milk and told him about the good stuff. The good stuff being the first date with his wife, the memories of small moments that imprinted a lasting impression on his heart and mind. The time he had married her, the times the laughed, loved, and cried. The time where they had children, raised them and then got grand babies. All of these small moments that pass by so quick and become lasting memories... The good stuff. So I say the following:

Make Time Count, What I mean by this is that we all need our own time, even if it's just a small amount we have to offer. My wife once told me something that inspired her about her dad. She said her dad didn't have much time with her and his kids growing up, but the time he did have with his kids, he made it count. See this goes to show you that even "Every other weekend" parents can have a huge impact on their kids, and that even if both a husband and a wife do have to spend a lot of time apart, when you do get together make it count and suck every single second into your life like a dry sponge. Do you know what her favorite song is? Play it for her over dinner. Do you know what his favorite food is? Make it for him while he is there. Thinks of it all and do it while you have the chance because it will never be known if you have another chance in the future. Live for the moment, climb mount Everest! I know I am being extreme but I really need you to know to make your time with your spouse count as much as you can. Have fun, make memories, and live life to the fullest.

As I stated in a previous chapter, Mommy and Daddy need time where just mommy and daddy go do something or get away, date nights, movies. Don't stop dating each other in your marriage. It is often seen that most couples stop dating once the marriage deed is done. Now that you are now married doesn't mean that your spouse does not deserve the same care and soft handedness with which you treated each other before your marriage. If anything, we should do more of those in marriage. Send her flowers at work just like you used to when you courted her. Call her to know if she needs anything during the day before leaving work from home. Buy her gifts upon your return from business trips and with every opportunity you get. Appreciate her cooking. Meet him in the doorway and welcome him back from work. Welcome him with a big hug and a kiss. Make him those candle light dinners that would pleasantly surprise and please him. Never take anything for granted because it is coming from your spouse. If anything, just as you would appreciate a colleague, friend or neighbor doing you a favor; do more in showing appreciation to your spouse in the simplest of things. This will encourage you both to do more and appreciate spending time together.

Just like mommy and daddy need mommy and daddy time, Mommy needs just time for herself and daddy needs just time by himself as well. This is important. In the days of courtship, you didn't do everything together. There were times you both had to do things you just had to do alone. You were not always on the phone with each other non-stop. That hasn't changed now as well. There may be times when either one of you may need to just be by oneself to think or just do one's own thing. For instance, daddy may just want to go play golf at the golf course by himself. Mummy might want to just sit back alone in the bedroom and knit for some time. The kids as well may sometimes just want to ride around the compound in their bicycles without interference from their parents.

There also has to be family time as well, where the whole family gets to be with each other and cherish in a love feast. Make time count. Go family camping, picnicking or something, just make sure that there are times the family just spends together that are always such sweet memories. In hard times, memories of the good times do reinforce togetherness and assure that things have not always been so and will not remain same but can only get better. This is very important to the psyche of the children. When the family is out together on an outing, it provides an awesome avenue for the husband and wife to be together in the presence of their children. While we may not be apt to notice, the children are however watching how mum and dad are seated together interacting. Being awesome learners, they pick up everything they see their parents do. They would learn same and are more likely to handle their spouse and family with same love when the time comes if they see such in their parent's marriage.

Chapter 6

"The Word is the World!"

Psalms 119: 103-105

[103] How sweet are thy words unto my taste! yea, sweeter than honey to my mouth!

[104] Through thy precepts I get understanding: therefore I hate every false way.

[105] Thy word is a lamp unto my feet, and a light unto my path.

Romans 10: 17

[17] So then faith cometh by hearing, and hearing by the word of God.

In the Bible, it is stated that "Faith comes by hearing and hearing comes by the word of God." The Bible is what feeds our spiritual man, and it's important for the union of husband and wife to dine together to feed their souls. In marriage, two become one and the husband being the head should take the lead in teaching and studying the bible with the wife. He is a spiritual head as well as the head of the home and should exhibit spiritual maturity and knowledge to be able to impart knowledge of the scriptures with the help of the Holy Spirit. It is easier to support one another in faith when a couple studies the bible together as you both can easily refer each other to a study period or topic that is relevant to your situations. This also ensures that the couple grows together in the spirit. This way both spouses can reinforce each other in times when the devil will come with temptations that could otherwise make either of you miss a couple beats. Remember in the Gospels we read that Stan went to tempt Jesus in the wilderness. The Devil did it with a cunning twist of the word of God, but the actual Word of God (Jesus Christ, The word incarnate) defeated Satan by reinforcing the "Truth" of the Word of God. Whenever he was tempted, Jesus would say, "Satan, for it is written!!!" He didn't have time for the devils tricks so he just said, "Boy, you just better back off, because this is the Word and the Word is the ultimate say so in this universe!"

We as Christians need to realize that the devil will come between us in our marriages by twisting facts, perverting the truth, and downright lying to a weak mind, but the good news is when a Christian marriage is founded on the Word of God, it cannot fail because in these times both of you know the "REAL TRUTH." You guys won't have time to believe the lies of the enemy, the perverted Gospel of a man or another women led by Satan to destroy your marriage. Do you want to know something awesome? Ill let you in on a secret I learned long ago. Satan is very, very, very afraid of a marriage to work out because he knows there is power in the union of soul mates believing together, walking together, and being together. If you look all the way back in Genesis you can see that Satan never tried to take down Adam or the Garden until Eve was in the picture. Once the serpent knew that there was a powerful bond that could destroy him and his demons he couldn't wait to tear it apart, and he did tear it apart, but often I wonder what would have happened if Adam had responded to the Serpent like Jesus did? What would have happened if Adam told the Serpent, or even Eve when she tempted him, "But God has said this serpent!!!" OF course what we are lead to believe is that they would have stayed safe in paradise. The Devil would love nothing more than to tear your marriage apart, so we must be ready to fend him off and get him out of our hair. We must be ready to discern the traps and lies he is laying for us in our paths. The only way to do so, is by knowing the Word of God.

How many times has a women advanced on a married man? Or, how many times has a man made an advance on a married women? It happens subtly. Maybe at first with a compliment, then a text, maybe even a phone call. The downward spiral starts there and it can only be stopped by a man or women who knows the word and can recognize it for what it is. I am going to be very truthful here. The point of this book was to bring reality and the Word of God together by explaining the cold hard facts, and the truth. I had an encounter once, as a married man where a women at work was going through a hard time, needed some advice, knowing that I was a pastor, she immediately came to me. Of course it wasn't her intention to get "Help" or "Consolation" from me, but rather other things. It started with advice, then moved to text messages, phone calls and one day my wife took note of it, and let's just say she put a stop to it right away. The point is, I was blinded to it by my love for people, she knew exactly what was going on, from the outside looking in, she knew the Word of God and because of that she was able to not only warn me of certain things that were going on, but we ended up avoiding what could have been a huge mess and a potential end to our marriage. I thank God for my wife knowing the Word of God, the same way there have been circumstances (Not as extreme) that I have been able to warn her of because when one partner of the marriage is down, the other stands strong.

The Bible says that merry is the man who walks with a friend because when he falls down, the other can pick him up, and a three cord strand is not easily broken. When we are down, our partner is up. When we are up are partner may be down, so we must pick them back up, but get this... When we add in the Word of God we make it a three cord strand, because we have brought God into the marriage. I want to show you a nice illustration that I learned a while back, look at the following picture:

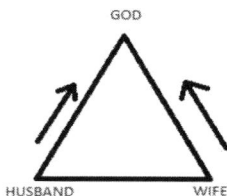

Do you notice something great? Of course you see a triangle with God at the top, and the husband and the wife at the bottom. Now check this out... If the husband and wife were to start following the arrows moving towards God, you would notice that the closer that the husband and wife Got to God, the closer they would be moving to each other as well. Kind of neat right? I call that the Great Marriage Triangle! So if you are both reading your word, searching out Gods will, and building your faith, you will naturally get closer, and closer, and closer to your spouse.

Another awesome thing about reading God's Word together is that it turns into deep, intimate conversations. Some of the most meaningful and miraculous conversations I have had were all based on talking about the word of God. I often use my wife as a white board for my sermons, she doesn't understand how much she is helping me by discussing my sermons with me, but to me she is being the biggest help I need at the time. It is an amazing thing on what the Lord can do within a marriage when the husband and wife base it on the Word of God.

Chapter 7

"Pray, Pray, Pray!"

Matthew 18: 18-20

[18] Verily I say unto you, Whatsoever ye shall bind on earth shall be bound in heaven: and whatsoever ye shall loose on earth shall be loosed in heaven.

[19] Again I say unto you, That if two of you shall agree on earth as touching any thing that they shall ask, it shall be done for them of my Father which is in heaven.

[20] For where two or three are gathered together in my name, there am I in the midst of them.

My Great Grandfather wrote a song called, "Pray, Pray, Pray." It talked about the importance of prayer and had a catchy old fashion country rock tune to it. To this day it is one of our Church congregations favorite songs he ever wrote. It went,

"When I get the blues, I'm going to take it to the Lord in Prayer. When I get the blues I'm going to take it to the Lord in Prayer. Because he said if I bring it to him, he would promise that he would always care!"

"Pray, Pray, Pray! Pray to him night and day, ohhh oh ohhh Pray, Pray, Pray! Pray to him right away!"

My Grandfather "Bob" Had found a way to comically, and clearly get across the point that you must always pray. There may be times in our marriages where we are struggling to stay strong, we may get depressed but if we pray to our Savior, we will find that he always cares.

I think I brought up an old saying earlier in this book that states, "A family that PRAYS together, STAYS together. The same is true in your marriage, if you pray with each other; you will stay with each other. When we pray, pray out loud with your spouse and be honest to God in front of your spouse about your hard times, difficulties, shortcomings and ask for forgiveness and help. This heals broken marriages. A prayer of agreement is also a strong supplication. Just as we should agree with our spouses in all things, we should agree with our spouses in prayer. Intercede for each other in the place of prayer just as Jesus urged his disciples and as Paul told the early disciples to do for one another. Let the place of prayer be a place where the plans of the family are brought before God. I encourage that couples hold hands, or even just touch each other somehow and pray out loud. I know this is hard for some people. I know a few people who praying out loud is difficult for them but this is crucial. I have told a few people who have come to me for advice that if you are embarrassed about praying with one another, ly down in bed and turn your backs to one another but let your backs touch each other, this way you stay touching one another in an intimate way, now while not facing each other but still touching back to back, pray out loud and be honest with one another before God. Pray about all your problems with your spouse. Let each person take turns soliciting the power of the Holy Spirit in the marriage.

PLEASE, PLEASE, PLEASE, remember that prayer time should never be a time where we tell God what to fix in our spouses lives. NO! God forbid because this would only bring up more frustration, and guilt, but rather pray about your own life. Your own shortcomings. God answers humble prayer, the prayer to change our lives and not the lives of another. We must always bring up our own faults and failures in our lives, not our spouses because you can only work on being the best husband you can be. You can only work on being the best wife you can be. You cant start being the artist who tries to chink out the imperfections from your spouse. God is the only potter that can mold the clay so let him do it without any help, he only needs you to help him with yourself.

Chapter 8

"Love Honor and Cherish."

Ephesians 5: 22-33

²² Wives, submit yourselves unto your own husbands, as unto the Lord.

²³ For the husband is the head of the wife, even as Christ is the head of the church: and he is the saviour of the body.

²⁴ Therefore as the church is subject unto Christ, so let the wives be to their own husbands in every thing.

²⁵ Husbands, love your wives, even as Christ also loved the church, and gave himself for it;

26 That he might sanctify and cleanse it with the washing of water by the word,

27 That he might present it to himself a glorious church, not having spot, or wrinkle, or any such thing; but that it should be holy and without blemish.

28 So ought men to love their wives as their own bodies. He that loveth his wife loveth himself.

29 For no man ever yet hated his own flesh; but nourisheth and cherisheth it, even as the Lord the church:

30 For we are members of his body, of his flesh, and of his bones.

31 For this cause shall a man leave his father and mother, and shall be joined unto his wife, and they two shall be one flesh.

³² This is a great mystery: but I speak concerning Christ and the church.

³³ Nevertheless let every one of you in particular so love his wife even as himself; and the wife see that she reverence her husband.

Respect and Honor Each Other. The Bible states for wives to submit to their husbands, and for the Husbands to love their wives as Christ loves the church and gave his life for it, so a husband should be willing to lose his life for the woman he loves but a woman should love her husband enough to submit to him, in big stuff and small stuff. It's important because of the way men and women are hard wired. A man just wants respect and honor, while a woman wants love and consideration because men are very

"Nuts and bolts" but women are like "thousands of computers in a warehouse with another tens of thousands of wires crisscrossing to each computer." Basically, men are kind of "Simple" and women are very "Complicated."

Men are very straight to the point and "fix it" set. Take for instance a situation where a wife takes her time to narrate an ordeal she went through perhaps at the store while picking groceries. A man keeps it simple, towards the end of the story, the man is more often than not, going to say a simple sentence or two suggesting a solution to what could have solved it all. Or you can see him saying, "There wasn't much you could have done to salvage the situation." It is quite different if the same were to be a conversation between two women. They can talk about a particular thing which would otherwise take men a few minutes to cap up, for way more than that, and they really have something going with the discussion. Women can spend two hours talking about the same subject when men just say a few things, change the subject, joke around and say "Yup, Yup." I can think of a hundred times my wife has come to me talking about a million things going on in her mind and my attitude towards it is, "How can I solve this right here, right now?" I then get so frustrated because there is no way for me to solve this situation in the moment so then my wife and I will argue and at the end of the conversation she will tell me, "Gosh Joey! I just wanted you to listen!" I think to myself, "Then woman why didn't you say so in the beginning!" It is so frustrating but I must be respectful to that because that just the way women are, and wives, be sensitive to the fact that everything you bring to your husband, he will auto automatically want to figure out a way to fix the problem, offer advice or give his opinion, so please be patient with his hard head before the argument starts. I remember a lady at Church telling me about a time she started yelling at her husband about things, life I assume, and her husband was obviously smarter than me because he asked her, "Hunny, is this one of those conversations where you just want me to listen?" She replied shaking her head up and down, "Yes." It is just the differences in our nature and we should understand this and respect each other's peculiar differences.

These differences are important and we can find its use when mothers take their time to listen to the chattering of their kids and be able to talk with them when they have things to say; in the way mothers talk to their babies who are yet only able to babble in inaudible ways that only the two of them can understand. It would be rare to see men who do not have such patience naturally. I mean, men can tolerate it and when tempered with the gift of the Holy Spirit can make quite a good run with it but the natural man is not built that way.

Show your wife that you love her. Thus has the bible commanded? Right? Love our wives like Christ loved the Church? Loving her is like watering a rose. You will see her blossom and flourish but if you don't, it may wilt and you can expect to get bitterness and rejection. The man desires to be respected and will not take being trampled upon. Speak to him gently and make your opinions known some way that he can understand and he may yet listen. Command or yell at him and you may have to wait a rather long wait, if he actually does decide to do your bidding, that is. I was told a piece of advice about this which is very, very true. A mentor of mine once told me that if you speak to the king in your husband, then you will reap a king but if you constantly speak to your husband like he is an idiot (Even if he is) then you will always reap the fool. Treat others the way you wish to be treated. I was told of a story where a minister went to dinner with his friend, his friend's wife was putting out all the fine china for dinner and he told her, "You didn't have to do this for me." She told the minister, "I didn't do it for you, I did it for my husband because he deserves the best every night." Amazing concept. I know this isn't realistic but it goes to show you what a wife or a husband putting each other first can come up with to show each other their love.

One thing we must remember about the Biblical scripture I brought up which says, "Wives submit to your husbands, and husbands love your wives." Is that if one person in the relationship isn't holding up their end of the bargain, it doesn't mean that the other person in the relationship should stop holding up their end of the bargain. I have heard it before, wives yelling at me in counseling sessions, "I am not submitting to that man because he doesn't love me!" and then, the husband yells out, "How can I love her when she doesn't submit to me!" Wow I thought to myself as I wanted to write down in the notes, "I know why this isn't working!" I didn't really write that down but I did tell them that whether he shows his love or not, it is the wives Godly responsibility to submit to her husband, and then I told him, whether she submits to you or not, it is still your Godly responsibility to LOVE YOUR WIFE!!! Do you see my frustration on this subject? We are taught by our own minds that if somebody doesn't do their part, then we don't have to do ours. This is actually called spite, and it ruins relationships every second of every day.

With an understanding of how both sexes are wired it is really important and is as simply stated in the bible; a husband is to love his wife even as Christ loved the church, i.e. even unto death; may God help us in doing this. To love her when you are hurting, love her when she offends you again and again. Love her when she throws your love, efforts, and sacrifices in your face; yes, it does not say to love her when it is convenient; no, but same as Christ has loved us, the Church. Same as he has loved us and died to save a humanity that did not accept him.

And a wife should honor and respect her husband. A very admirable example from the Bible is Sarah, Abraham's wife. She calls her husband, Abraham her lord and follows him on a visionless journey to a land that a voice only Abraham can hear, tells him is his promise land. Kind of crazy by today's standards of psychotherapy right?

Chapter 9

"Communication is Key!"

Ephesians 4: 29

[29] Let no corrupt communication proceed out of your mouth, but that which is good to the use of edifying, that it may minister grace unto the hearers.

Communicate with your spouse. Talk to one another, over, and over, and over again. This mainly goes for women, I'll tell you why because us men are "Simple" and actually very "Stupid" at times. Our wives get mad at us because we forgot an important date… oops… How many of us men have done this? All! So wives, don't get mad, just remind him by communicating. I'm still learning this in my marriage. Once my wife told me out of nowhere… "Hunny I am going to be out of town for my business meeting next week." I all of a sudden was like "What?!?!?!" I began to get mad and asked her why she didn't tell me sooner and she told me, "Hunny I did tell you, 5 times over the past month!" Oh my, I felt horrible because she did tell me but I was so "Simple" minded that I forgot. Men need help, but women also need something more important than help… They need a person who will LISTEN. Listening is a huge part of communication so husbands really listen to your wife. Turn off the game, get off of the computer, close the book, Stop studying the bible (For those who are Pastors), tune everything out and just sit down and listen to your wife. It's so important. A listening ear is better than a mouth that flatters. Do not be too busy to listen to your spouse. Do not cut each other short, whether you think what is being said is rather long, important or not, do listen. That is what you both are there for each other for. Those little things that your spouse wants to talk to you about at those times that you think there are more important things to do, are most likely things she can't discuss with anyone else. If you reject her friendly conversation, then who would you rather should listen to her.

Women are naturally better at multi-tasking than we men. We understand you can juggle through a number of things at the same time and still be able to do what needs to be done at the specific time you should without abandoning the rest of what you are to manage; it's not just that easy for us men. We are more apt to focus on one task and get done with it before remembering that the other task which was processing at the same time is already overdue. Wives please do remind your husbands of the things he has agreed to do but has not yet done. Most times it is not because he just did not feel like doing it again; it probably just skipped his mind. Communication in these matters goes a long way to foster understanding.

Chapter 10

"Think on these things!"

Philippians 4: 6-8

[6] Be careful for nothing; but in every thing by prayer and supplication with thanksgiving let your requests be made known unto God.

[7] And the peace of God, which passeth all understanding, shall keep your hearts and minds through Christ Jesus.

[8] Finally, brethren, whatsoever things are true, whatsoever things are honest, whatsoever things are just, whatsoever things are pure, whatsoever things are lovely, whatsoever things are of good report; if there be any virtue, and if there be any praise, think on these things.

When the Church of Philippi received a letter from the Apostle Paul, in Chapter 4 he was telling them how to live in peace, with no worry and being anxious for nothing. He told them not to even begin to worry about things but instead pray about everything, and then he told them, just in case you find yourself starting to think about bad stuff that will make you worry, THINK ON THESE THINGS! He told them to think about the pure things, the pleasant things, the things of good report and good virtue. He said if there be any good, or any praise in something, then think about it and the God which gives peace will give us a peace that passes all understanding.

Many times in our marriage we find ourselves in a bad spot, maybe we have been through a round of arguments, or have said some things to one another that hurt really bad. Maybe you want to give up and quit. Maybe like some you find yourself taking off in a car, parking somewhere and stewing over EVERYTHING THAT HAS GONE WRONG? Maybe? Well this is where we are actually supposed to practice what Paul said and think about the good things. One tiny memory of a victory or a happy moment will overthrow any bad onslaught of depressing thoughts you might have. Remember when we were young, some of you may remember it, some may not, but there was a song we used to sing that said, "Count your blessings name them one by one." We really need to tally up the good points rather than keeping track of the bad ones all the time. If we are always making a big deal about the bad thoughts, then we are sure to be defeated, not just in our marriages but in our lives period. You will get frustrated and just want to give up. Let me give you an example. I worked in a youth group home that kept a list of points for each kid in the home. We were supposed to put a point on their chart every time they did something wrong. By the end of the day they would have amassed points based on how many bad things they had done that day. I was young and just did my job, writing down each incident and giving a point on each kids chart when they disobeyed or didn't complete a task. One kid was always getting tons of points and one day he came to me as I was marking down a point on his chart and he told me he was just going to give up. He didn't want to even try anymore. I thought to myself, "When has this kid even tried, he always has tons of points!?!?!" He obviously didn't care, at least I thought at that time. The next day I took him to his counselor and brought up the conversation about him wanting to quit, give up and even go to jail. He said he was treated more fairly in jail. The counselor asked him what he meant and the kid told him, "They always give me points for what I do wrong but they never pay attention to when I do something nice." The counselor asked me if this was true. I had to really think hard, but as I thought about it I remembered that this kid actually did go to school all the time. He picked up his cloths, did his homework and even did extra chores at times, but then I realized we never kept track of the good things these kids did, only the bad things. It was eye opening. This kid would have rather gone back to jail then in a clean, family oriented home with a warm bed and cable tv because at least in jail they gave him some praise for being good at times. The counselor then told me that this was a flaw in many group homes. The homes would only focus on bad behavior and never reinforced the good behavior which always led to the children acting out more, doing worse things, giving up and some even taking their own lives.

The same is true in our marriage. If we consistently tally up the bad then we are putting ourselves and our spouses in a no win situation. We constantly keep track of all the times our spouse hasn't done something which makes them frustrated like they aren't being listened too, or watched and it always winds up being a huge "Hurt Locker" for our spouses in which they just want to stop trying, or go find a person that notices these things they do. I see this in my own marriage on a daily basis. My wife and I are all too thrilled and prepared to remember the bad times, but my wife and I on a regular bases make a mental note to tally up the good. It is natural for our fallen, human minds to remember how people have hurt us, or didn't add up, rather than remembering the good things, the pure things, the true and virtuous things. We want to remember things like, He didn't take the trash out again. She didn't cook dinner. That jerk only thinks about himself, look, he even left the toilet seat up to prove it. He doesn't care, he never does this or he never does that. She never does this, or she never does that and then comes that moment where we think the grass might be greener on the other side and we think, "I wonder if that other girl would be like this?" or "I wonder if Kasey's Husband treats her this way?" Dangerous I will say, and it's the small thoughts like this that turn into adultery in our hearts. Instead we should remember the kid's birthday where he remembered they wanted that sponge Bob cake with the green center. Oh cool! He warmed up my car for me this morning. How nice that my wife cooked my favorite dinner for me tonight. Oh wow, she smiled that same way on our first date. He got my favorite flower, lit my favorite scented candle… Wait, he actually remembered what my favorite flower and candle is? These are the things that we should be thinking about, especially in times of turmoil and strife. The Bible promised that if you thought on these things then you would have a peace that passes all understanding. Think about it.

Chapter 11

"Committing to the Commitment!"

Ecclesiastes 5: 4-7 (New International Version)

[4] When you make a vow to God, do not delay to fulfill it. He has no pleasure in fools; fulfill your vow.

[5] It is better not to make a vow than to make one and not fulfill it.

[6] Do not let your mouth lead you into sin. And do not protest to the temple messenger, "My vow was a mistake." Why should God be angry at what you say and destroy the work of your hands?

[7] Much dreaming and many words are meaningless. Therefore fear God

Protect and Honor your marriage vows. Fight for your marriage! Don't take mediocrity at its finest, rather have the best, at all times! I tell married couples all the time… "You have to be committed to the commitment." Part of your marriage vows said "Till Death do us part." Not till lying does us a part, not until a messy house does us a part, and not until an argument does us a part, not even till cheating does us apart. I know this is so hard, but Jesus Christ has forgiven us of all sins, even spiritually cheating on him with other Gods, so we must be ready to forgive all sins in our marriages as well. It takes work, hard work. I never said that marriage was going to be easy or automatic. Those butterflies that you felt in the beginning turn into nausea and heartburn. Those bright eyes full of life turn into tears and trials, but when you make it work, it's worth more than its weight in Gold. Sometimes in our marriages we get to a point where we loathe our other half! I will be honest; I got to a point one time where I started throwing a fit because my significant other squeezed the toothpaste at the top instead of rolling it from the bottom. How pathetic right!? It happens though. Nothing will ever prepare you for marriage except being committed to the commitment once you are in the commitment (Catch that? Haha) but it's true. Marriage is one of those things that you have to learn as you go and have a trial by fire. Its Gods plan though. He knew we would never be able to get along 100 percent of the time this is why he tells us to forgive one and other, and when all else fails and you feel like running away and being done, calling it quits, you must remember your marriage vows and keep on going until things turn around. NEVER SAY THE "D" WORD (Divorce). Never run away in the heat of an argument, and NEVER let the sun go down on your wrath, hatred, or anger. Stay committed to the person you knew when you made those promises that stated, "In sickness and health, richer or poorer and till death do you part. Marriage is not fireproof. Sometimes it may burn you, but it is how you handle those little differences, trials, and tough times, and how you come through them that defines the course of your marriage. Remember this simple rule of thumb; "never to leave a partner in a fire" because your partner may yet be scouting for you, thinking that something may have happened to you. So when things are tough, it's not time to run. It's time to save one another because you are one. In hard times, hold onto each other and to God. You will find that you will both come out strong and enjoy an even deeper, more rewarding commitment to your marriage.

Your marriage vows are very binding and cannot be broken by man. It is not just about a marriage document that was issued to you both by the church, but the solemn promise which you both made before God that day. It is a life-long covenant. After that day, you don't do what pleases you alone anymore but rather every decision should consider your better half before self. MARRIAGE ISNT FOR YOU!

In no way, shape, or form was marriage ever for YOU, it was always for God to USE YOU TO BLESS ANOTHER. You both must stand together, always ready to forgive and excuse each other's shortcomings, to trust, to hope and to endure whatever comes.

"A Word from Pastor Joey."

I hope as you read this book that you not only enjoyed it, but you were able to learn something that can change you, your life, and your marriage. I never write these books to get famous, make tons of money, or any other ulterior motives, but rather, I write these books in hopes of healing hurting people, rebuilding broken homes and families, and hopefully inspiring some hope in the ones who pick up these books. I want it to be known that if somebody needs help in their walk with Jesus, then Comeback Kids Ministries will always be here to answer the call. I want to pass on the knowledge that God has given me in my times of need, so that others will have them in their times of need.

Please, if you liked this book go back to the Amazon page and LEAVE A REVIEW. You can go to the following link to leave a find all of the books from Comeback Kids Ministries:

www.pastorjoeybauer.org

I would also like to share some other links with you so you can find out more about us, write us a letter or even just follow us as a partner. If you want to "Like" us on Facebook you can find us at the following link:

www.facebook.com/cbk217

If you want to donate to our ministry, or would like to just find out more information about what we do, go to our official website at the following link:

www.comebackkids.webs.com

We would love to hear from you. We even have a Youtube site where we post sermons up from the Ministry, we are always looking for more people to like our videos and share them with others, in hopes of helping somebody through a difficult time in their life. Go to our Youtube page and check us out at the following link:

www.youtube.com/user/Comeb ackkidsministri

Comeback Kids Ministries

Thanks for the support, until next time my friends. Be blessed and be encouraged.

Comeback Kids Ministries Pastor Joey Bauer!!!

Made in the USA
Charleston, SC
14 March 2014